The Science of Bones 3rd Grade Textbook

CHILDREN'S BIOLOGY BOOKS

BABY PROFESSOR

EDUCATION KIDS

Speedy Publishing LLC

40 E. Main St. #1156

Newark, DE 19711

www.speedypublishing.com

Copyright 2016

Imagine humans having to move like a gelatinous jellyfish if they had no bones. Never forget to drink milk, as our mothers would always say. Milk is a major source of calcium, which is very important in bone development.

Sports and daily activities like walking, running, and jumping are movements enabled by the basic framework of the body: the bones.

SKELETON

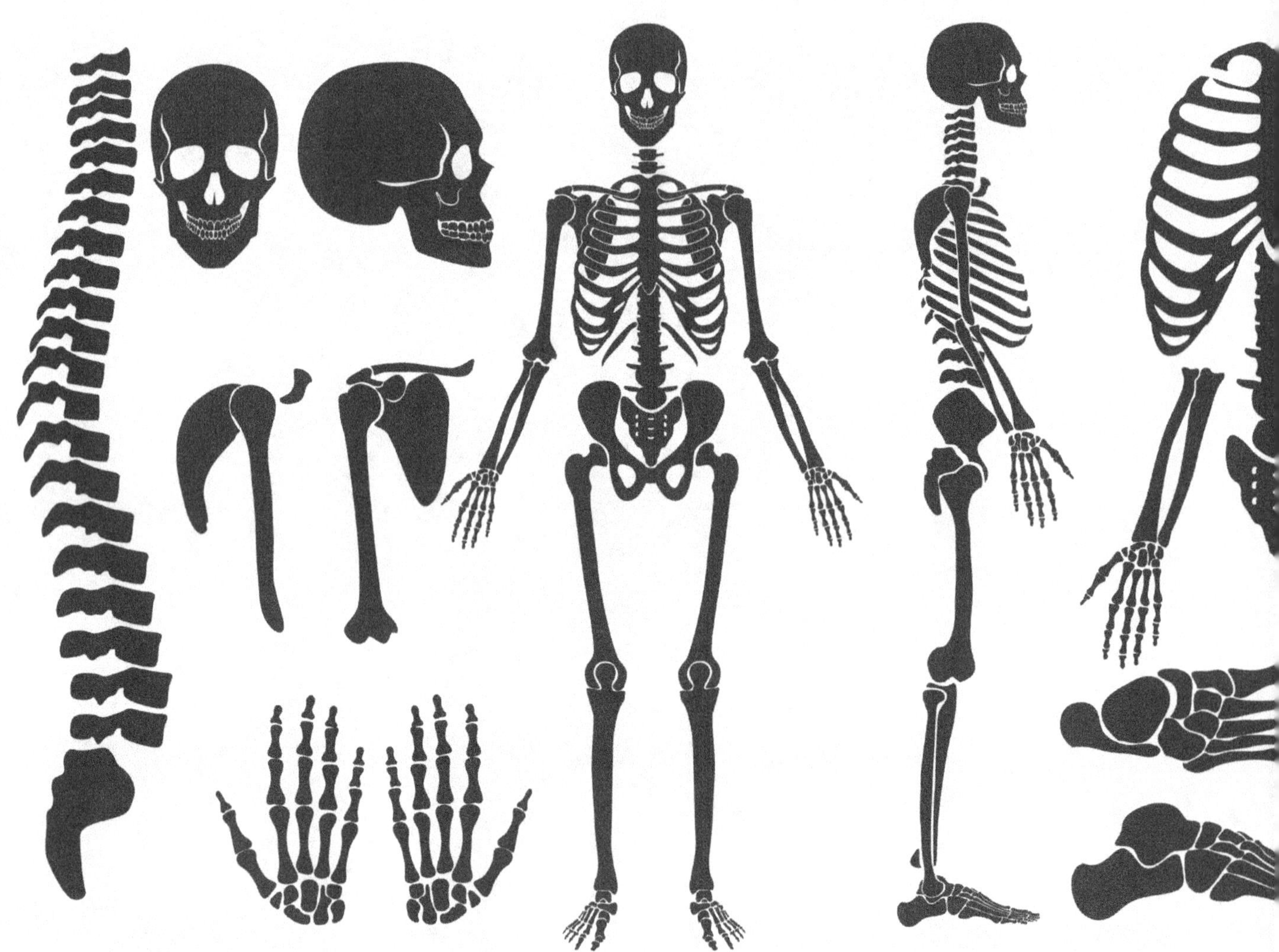

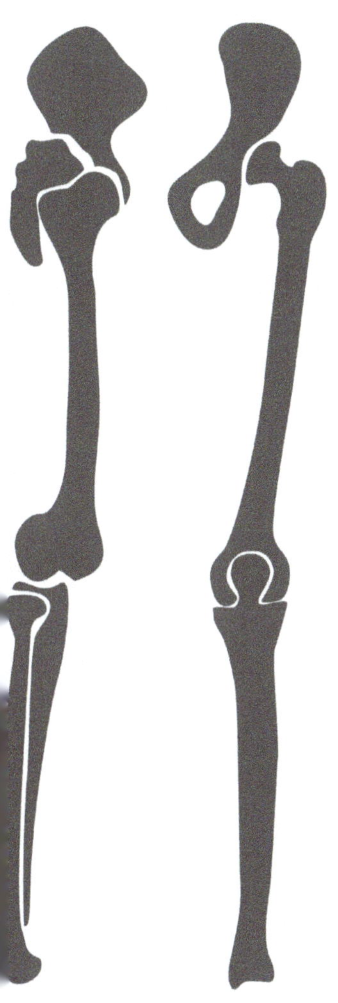

Bones come in different shapes and sizes. They serve as a framework which supports and protects the internal and external organs of the body.

The major reason why
the human body is able
to move is that bones
allow the muscles to
work.

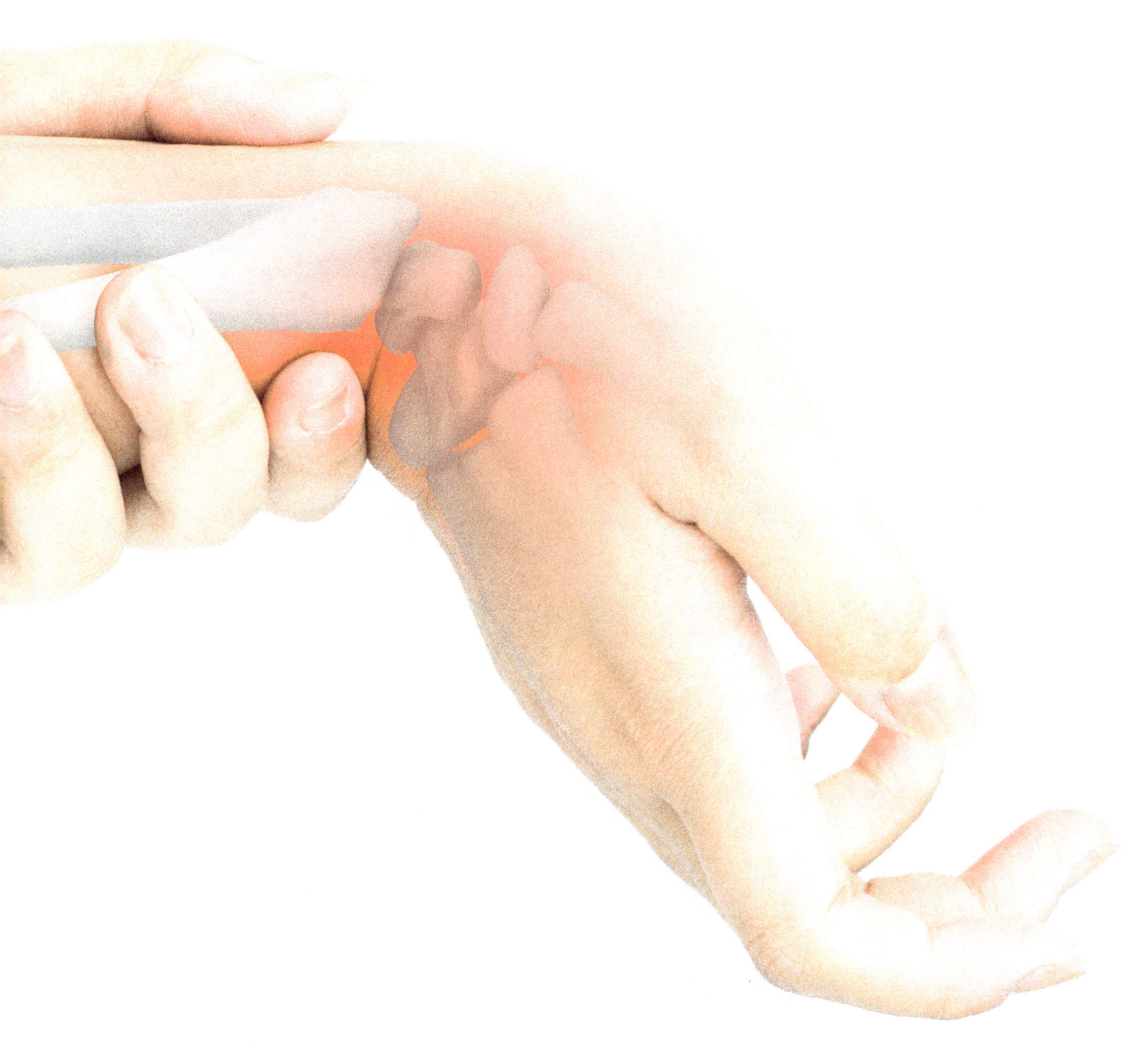

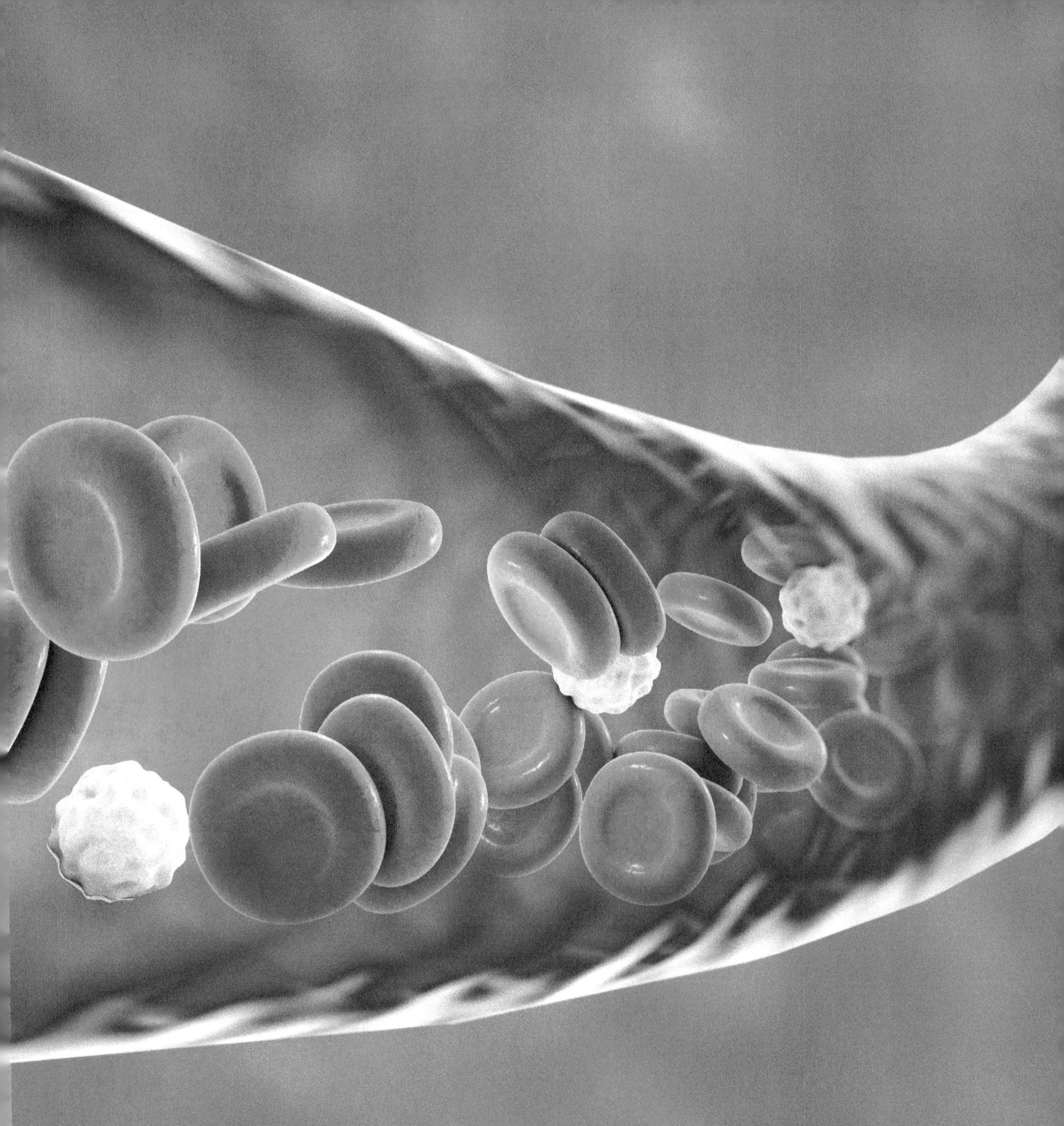

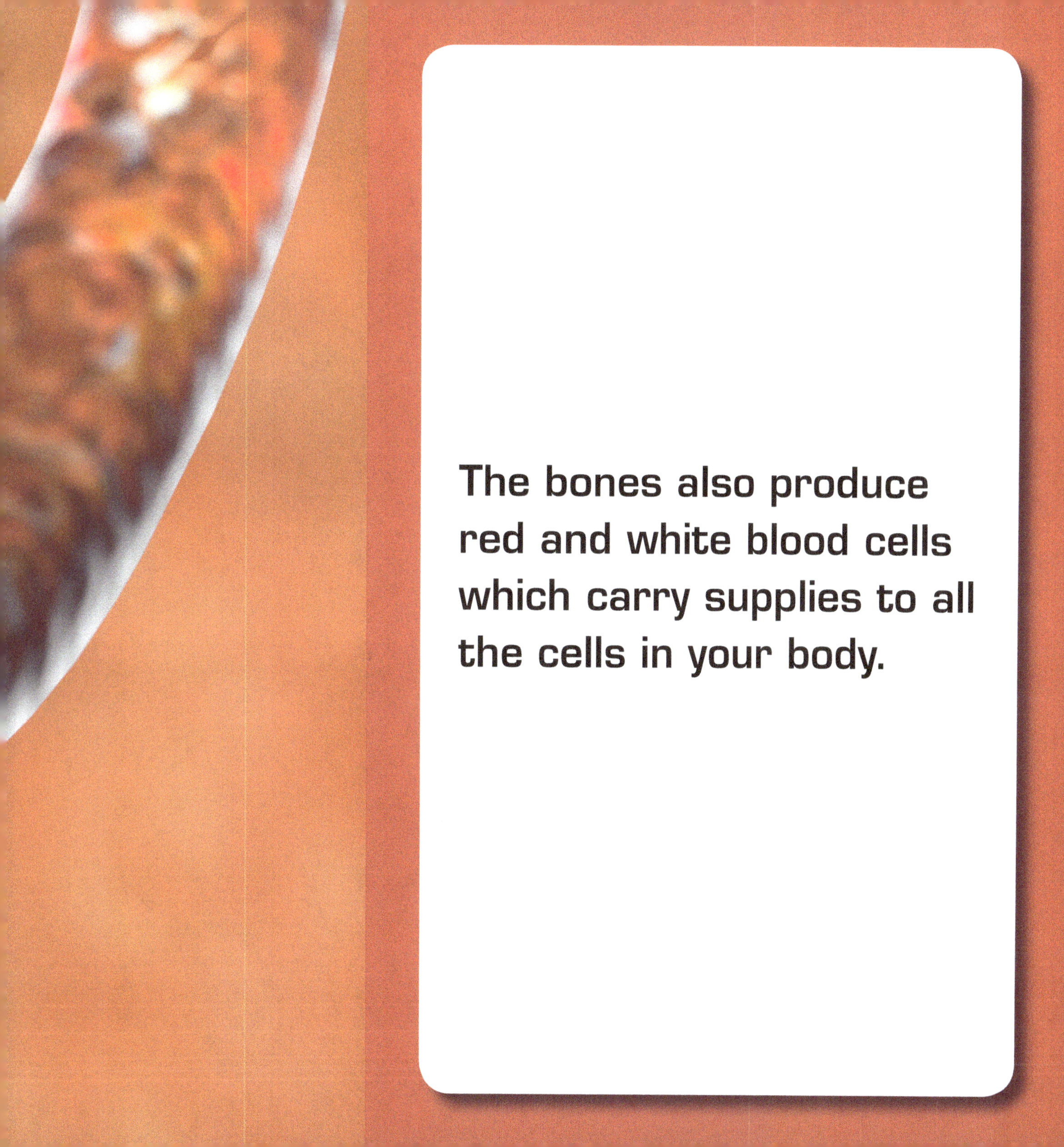

The bones also produce red and white blood cells which carry supplies to all the cells in your body.

Minerals are stored as bones grow. The human skeleton is composed of an average of 206 bones once it reaches adulthood.

HUMAN BONES

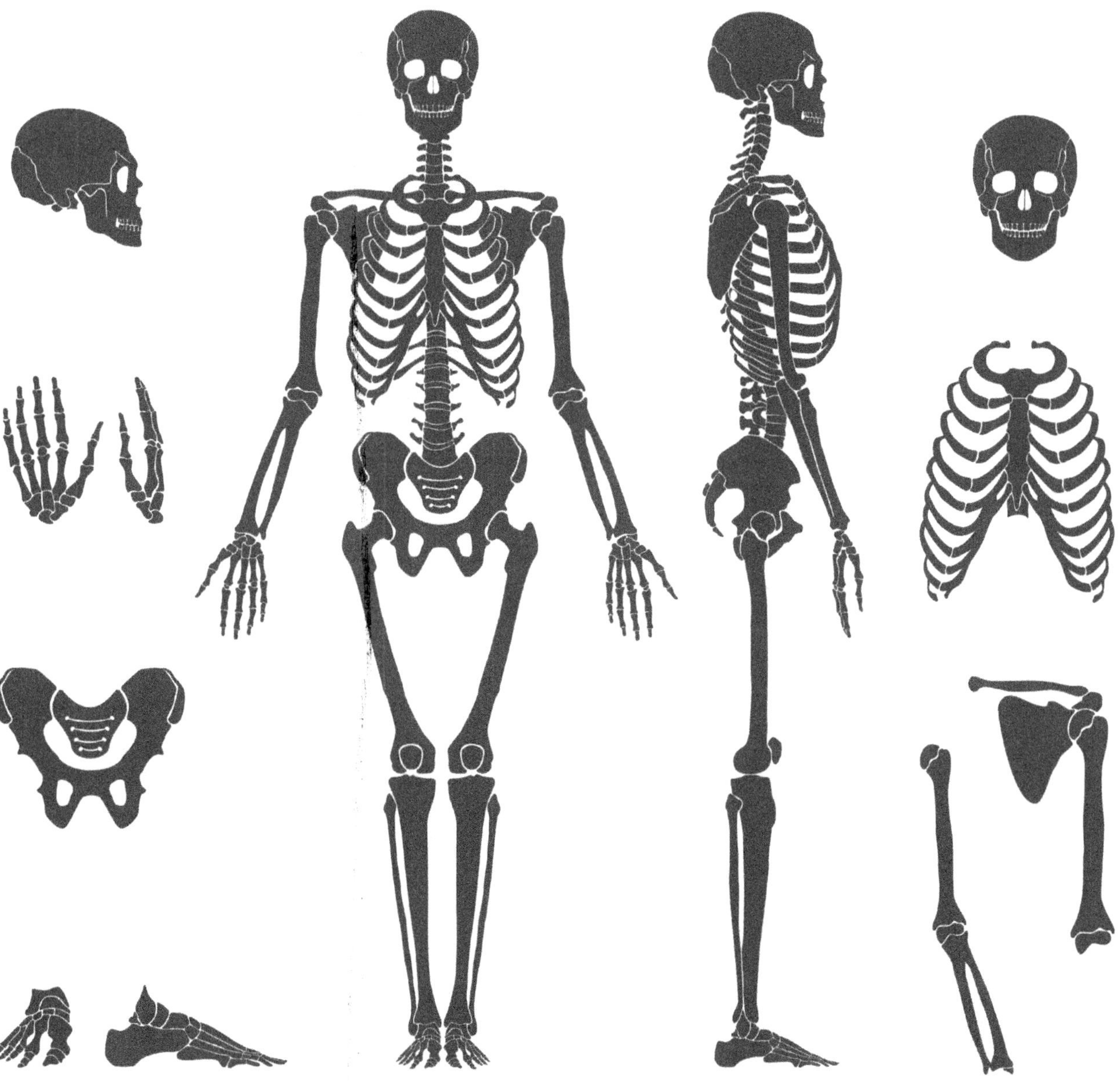

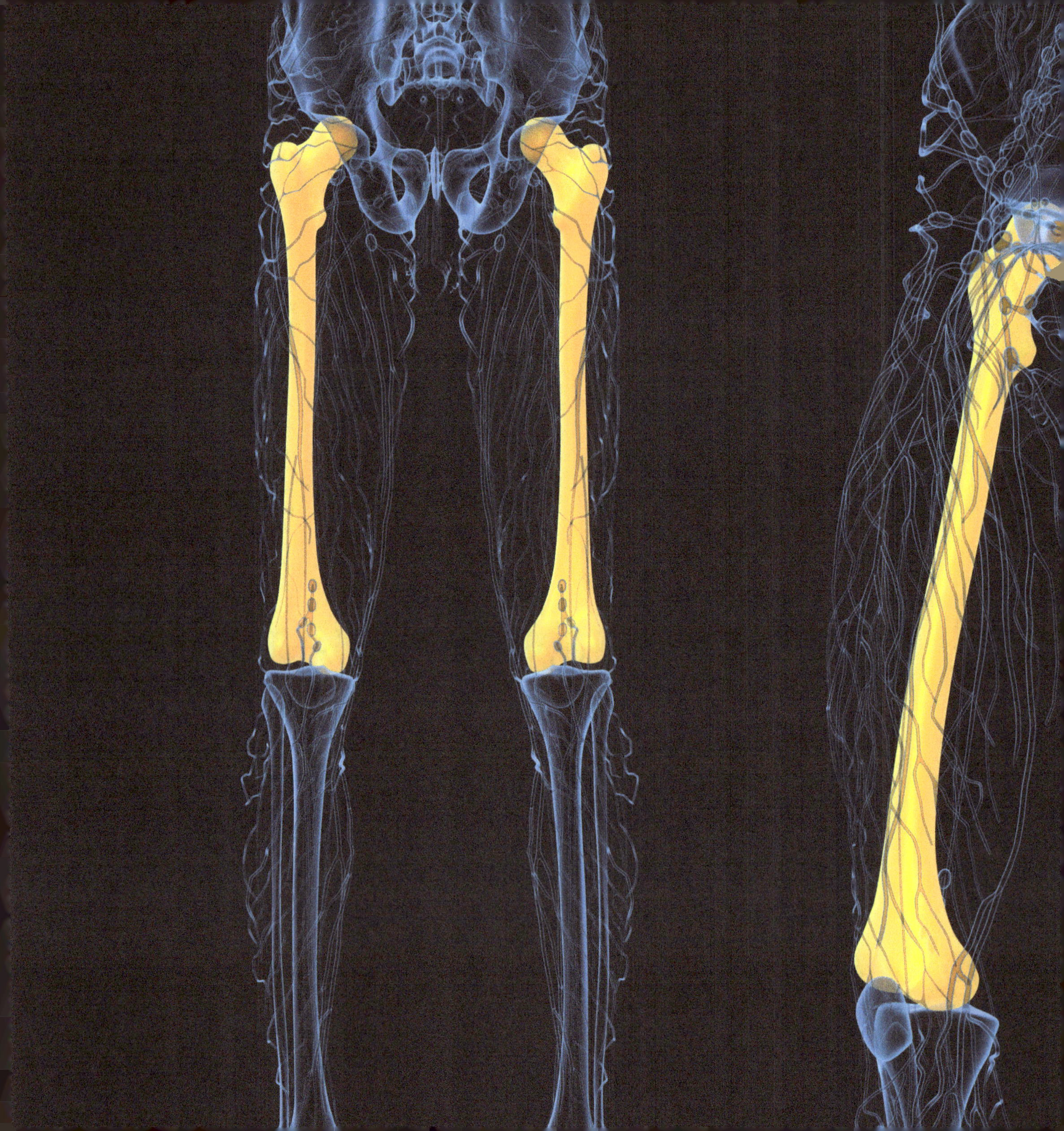

The strongest and longest bone is called the thighbone (femur). The bones located in the middle ears are the smallest and lightest bones, known as staples.

There is only one bone that is not connected to another—the hyoid. It is shaped like a V and located at the base of the tongue.

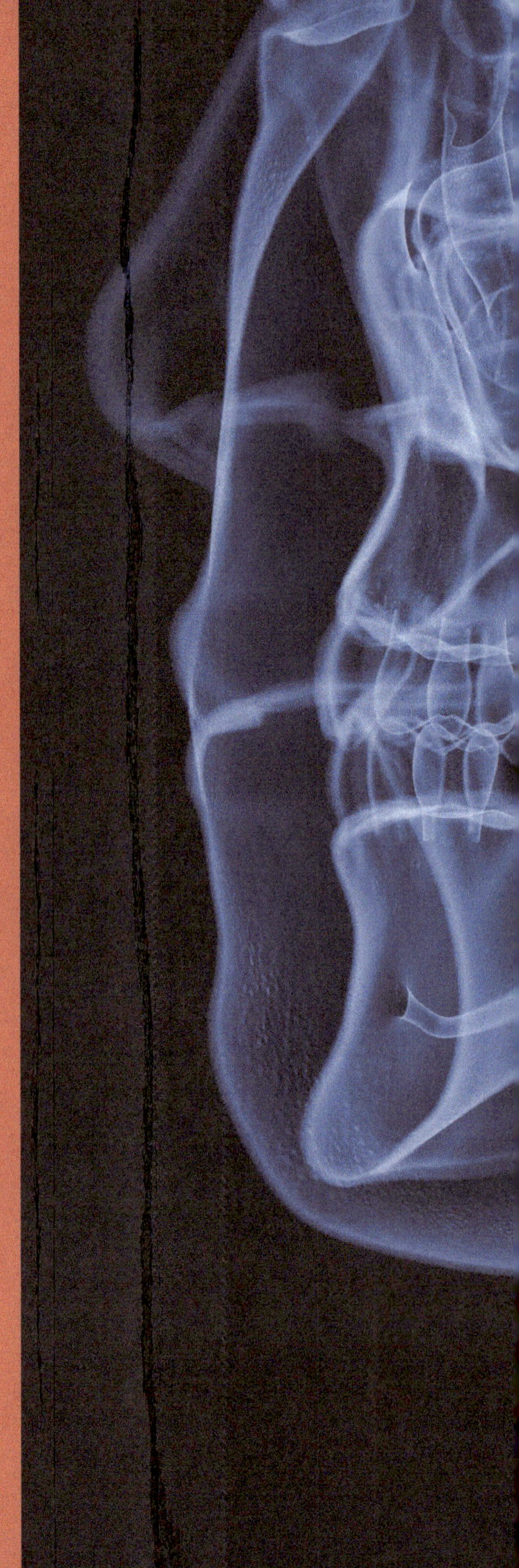

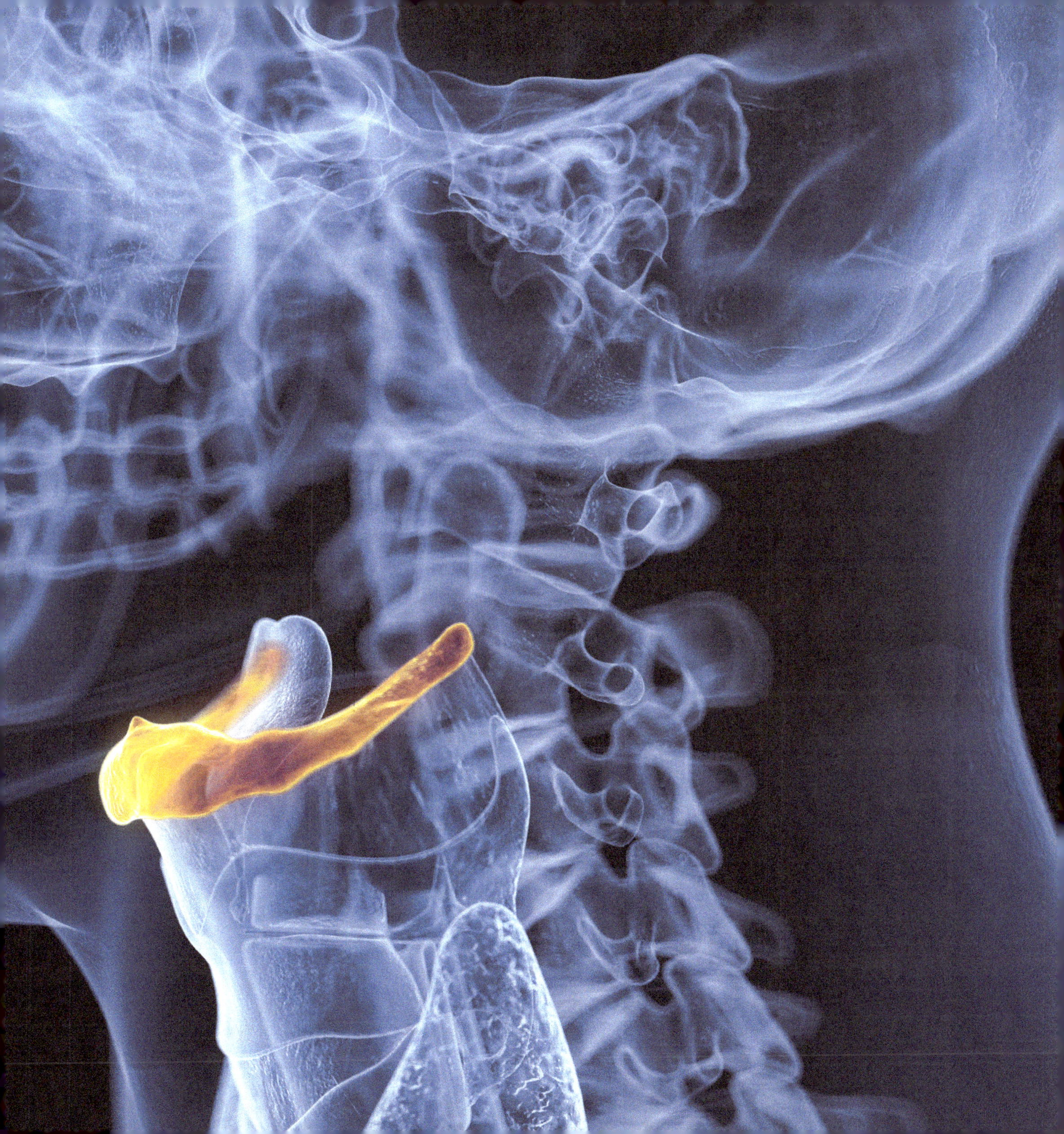

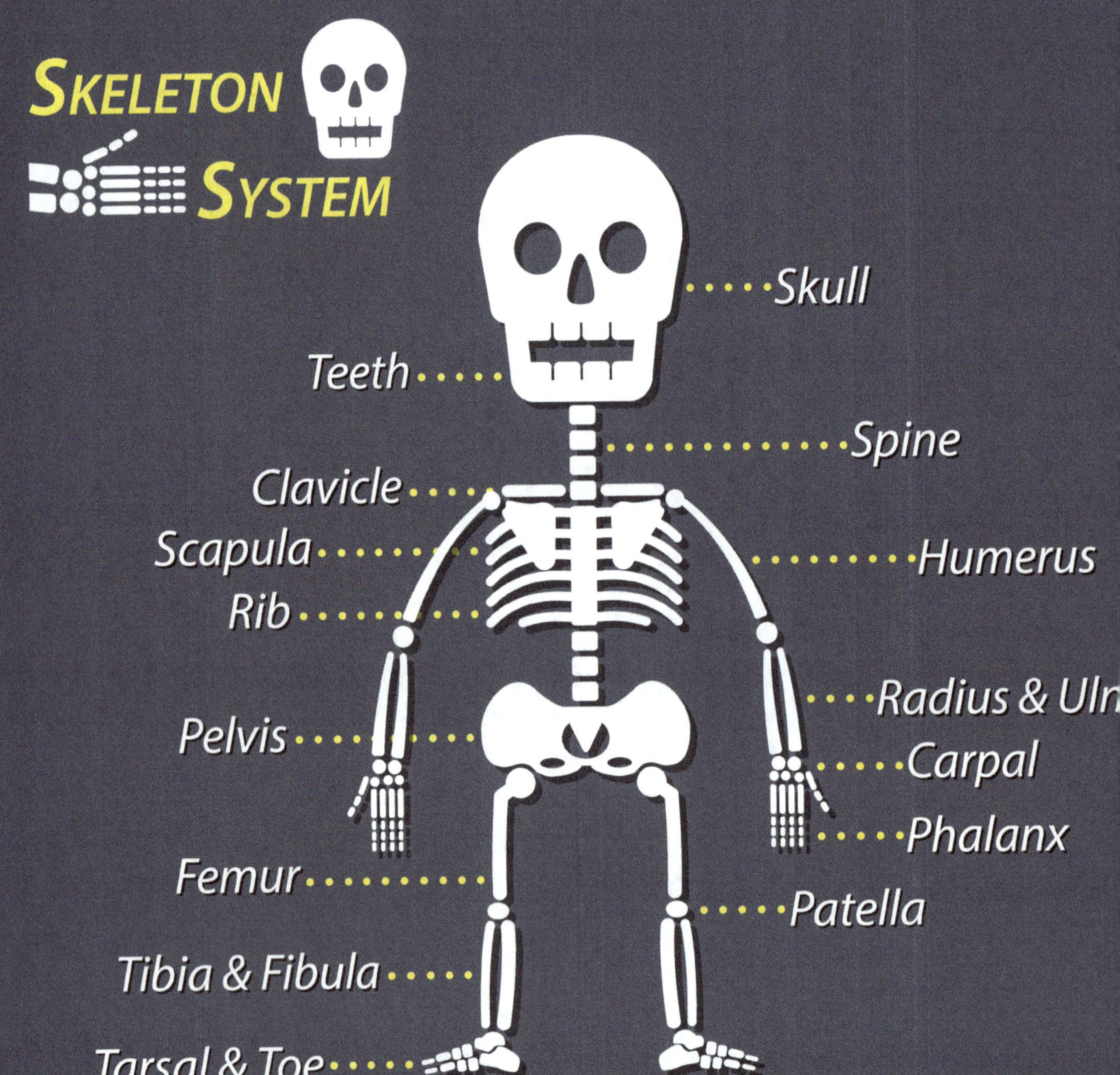

Skeleton System
Skull
Teeth
Spine
Clavicle
Scapula
Humerus
Rib
Radius & Ulna
Pelvis
Carpal
Phalanx
Femur
Patella
Tibia & Fibula
Tarsal & Toe

There are other major bones of the human skeletal system. Let's identify them one by one, from head to toe. Each has a specific function as it grows in density, length, and strength.

The **skull** or **cranium** encloses the brain. Down to the shoulder blade. The **collar bone** or **clavicle** connects with the breastbone.

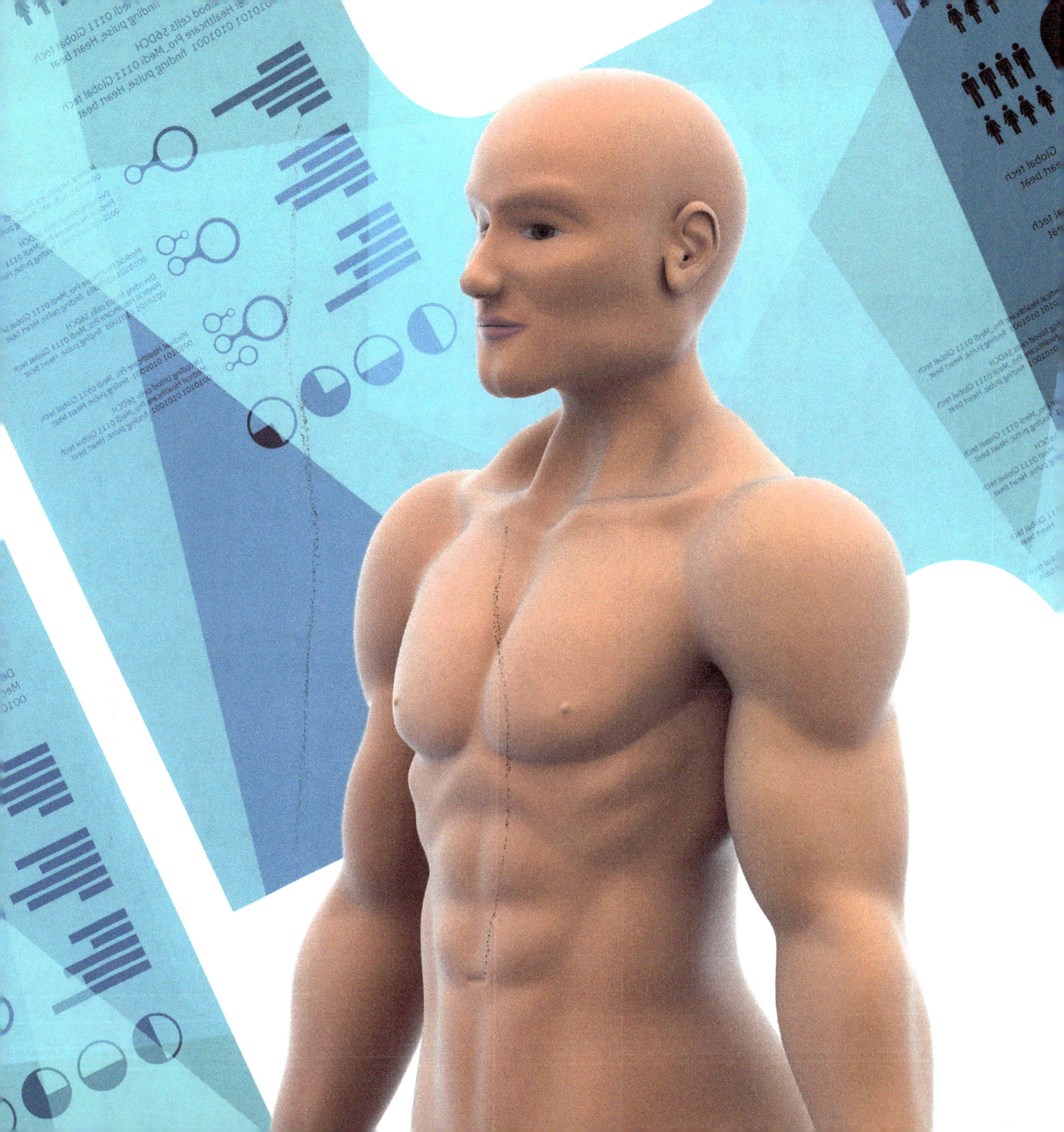

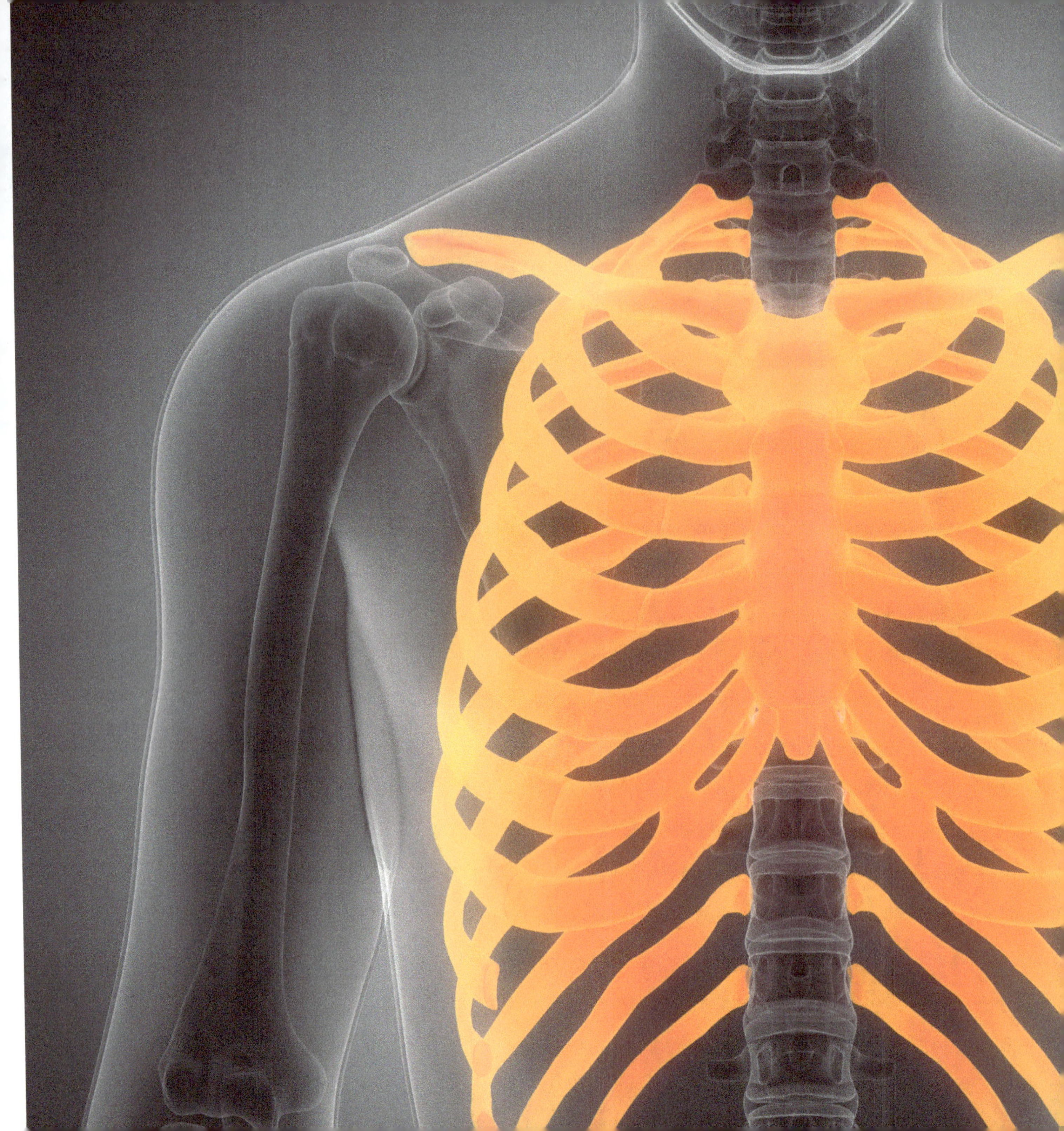

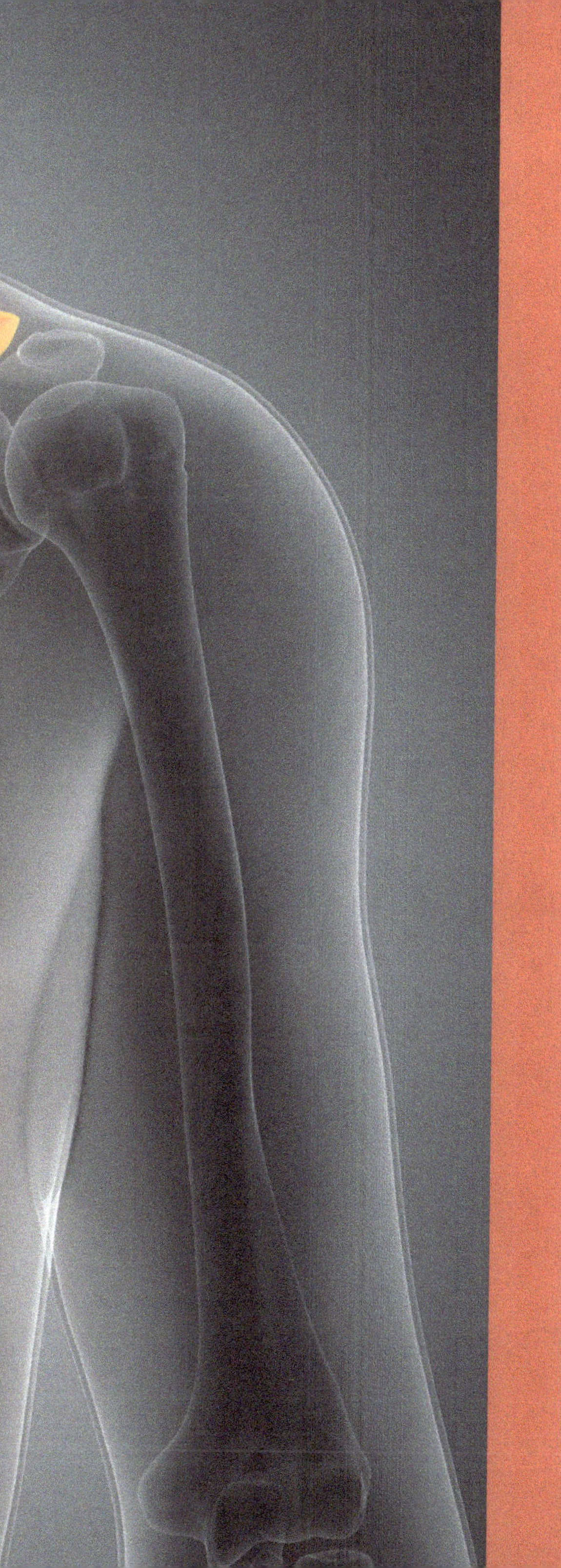

Ribs are long curved bones which form the rib cage of the chest. These come in pairs jointly from the spinal column. The rib cage keeps the major internal organs of the body protected.

The spine, also known as the backbone, is made of sections (vertebrae) that have the spinal canal in the middle, protecting the spinal cord.

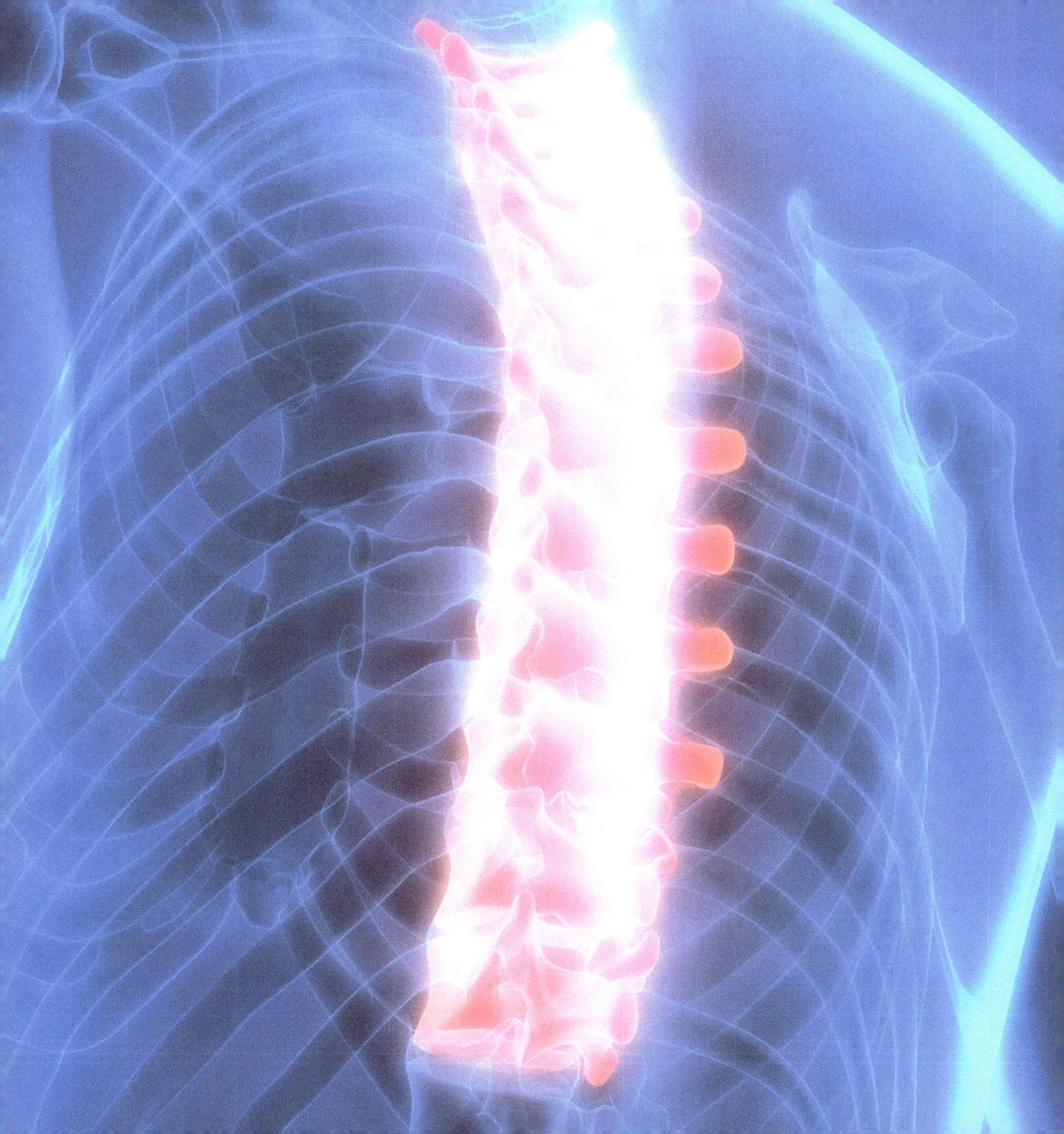

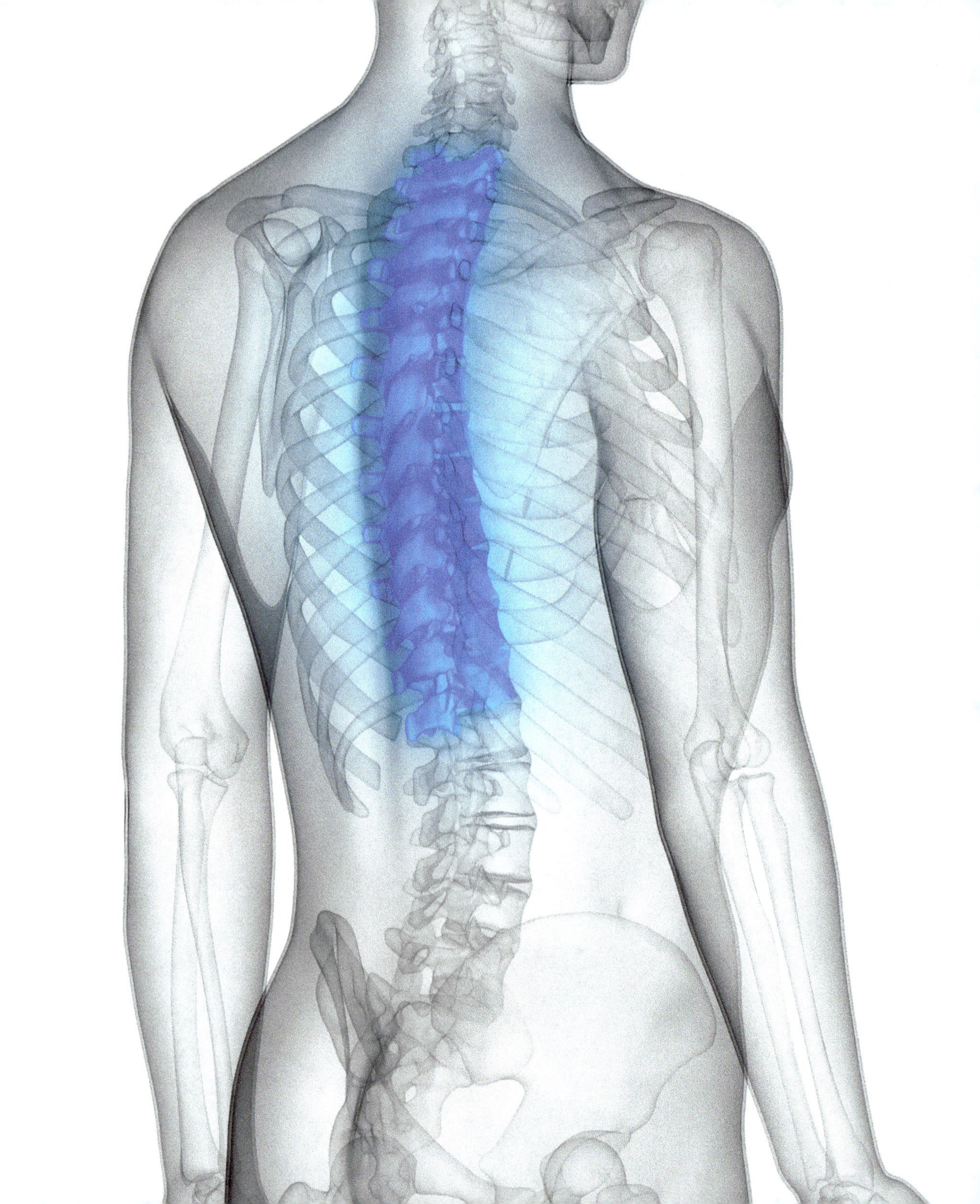

Between the neck and abdomen is part of the spine called the thoracic vertebrae (upper spine). Right below the lower ribs and hips are the lumbar vertebrae (lower spine).

The bone from the elbow to the wrist (thumbside of the forearm) is known as the radius. The bone on the pinky finger side (lower arm) is called the ulna.

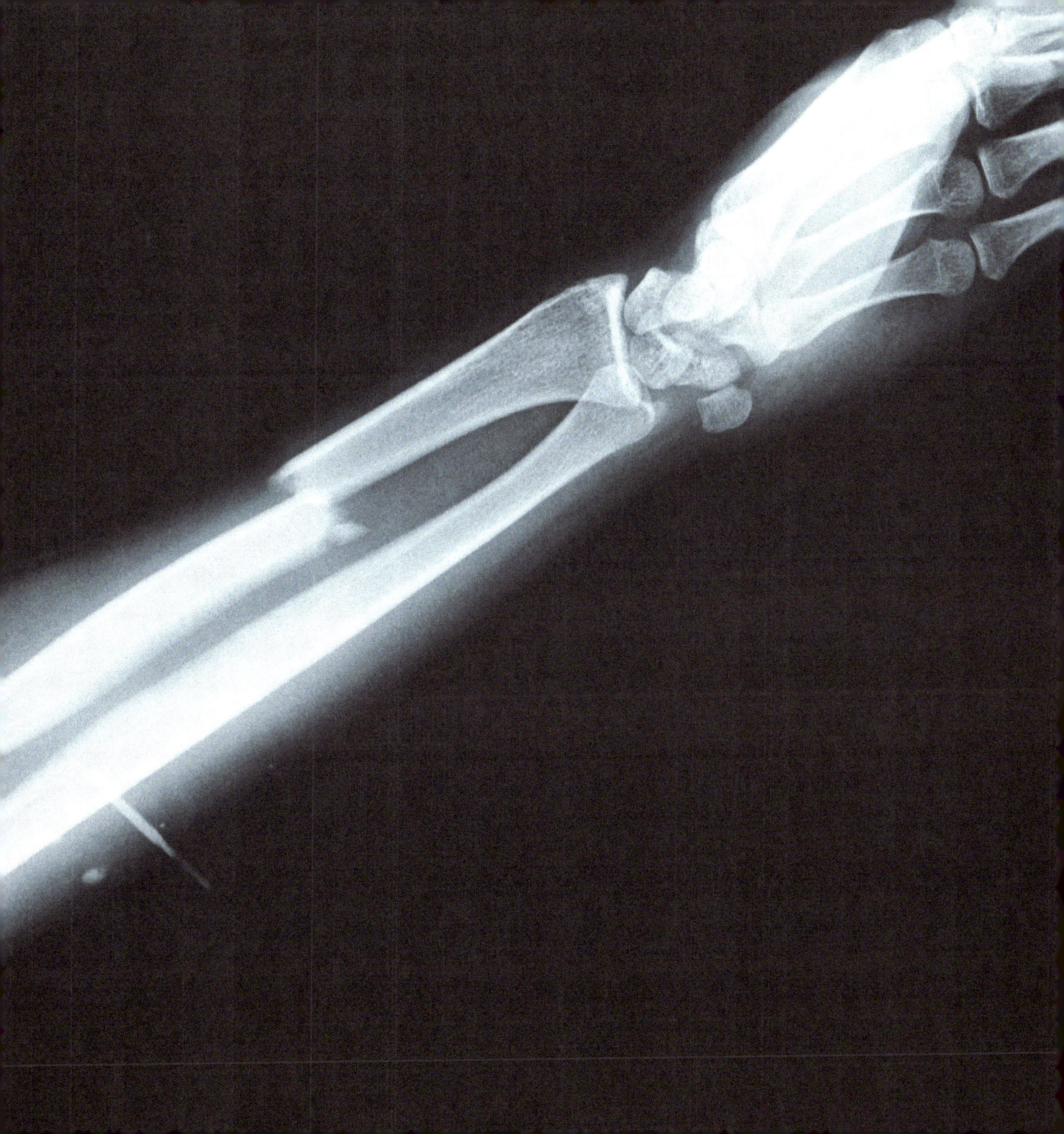

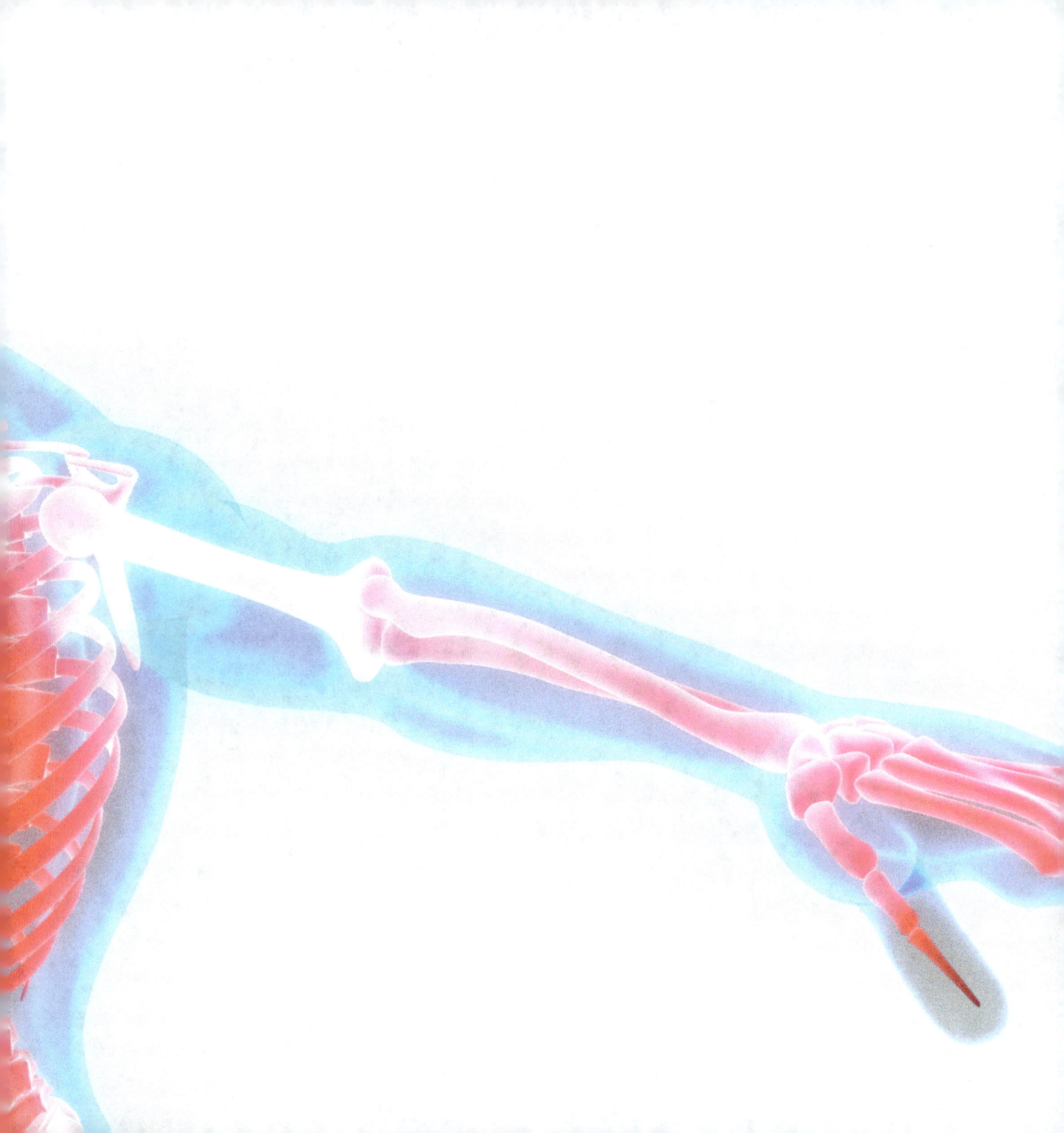

Humerus is the long bone of the upper arm from shoulder to elbow. Those tiny bones of the fingers or toes are called **phalanges**.

The hip bone or pelvic girdle is shaped like an arc that supports the torso and connects with the legs.

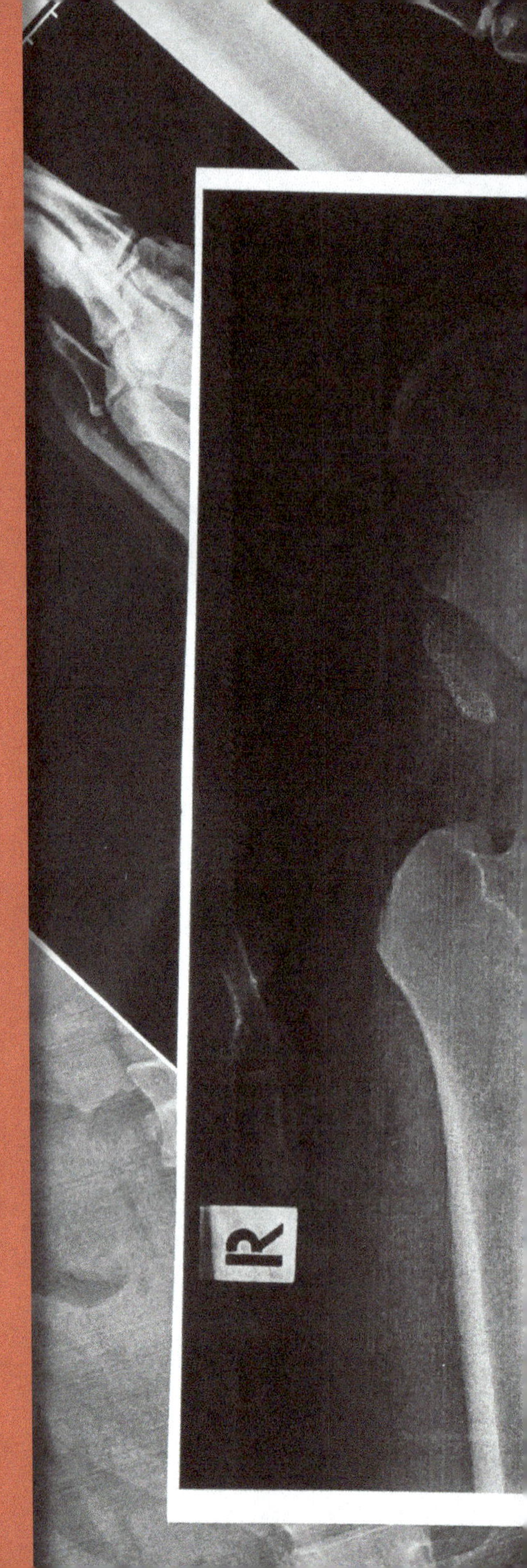

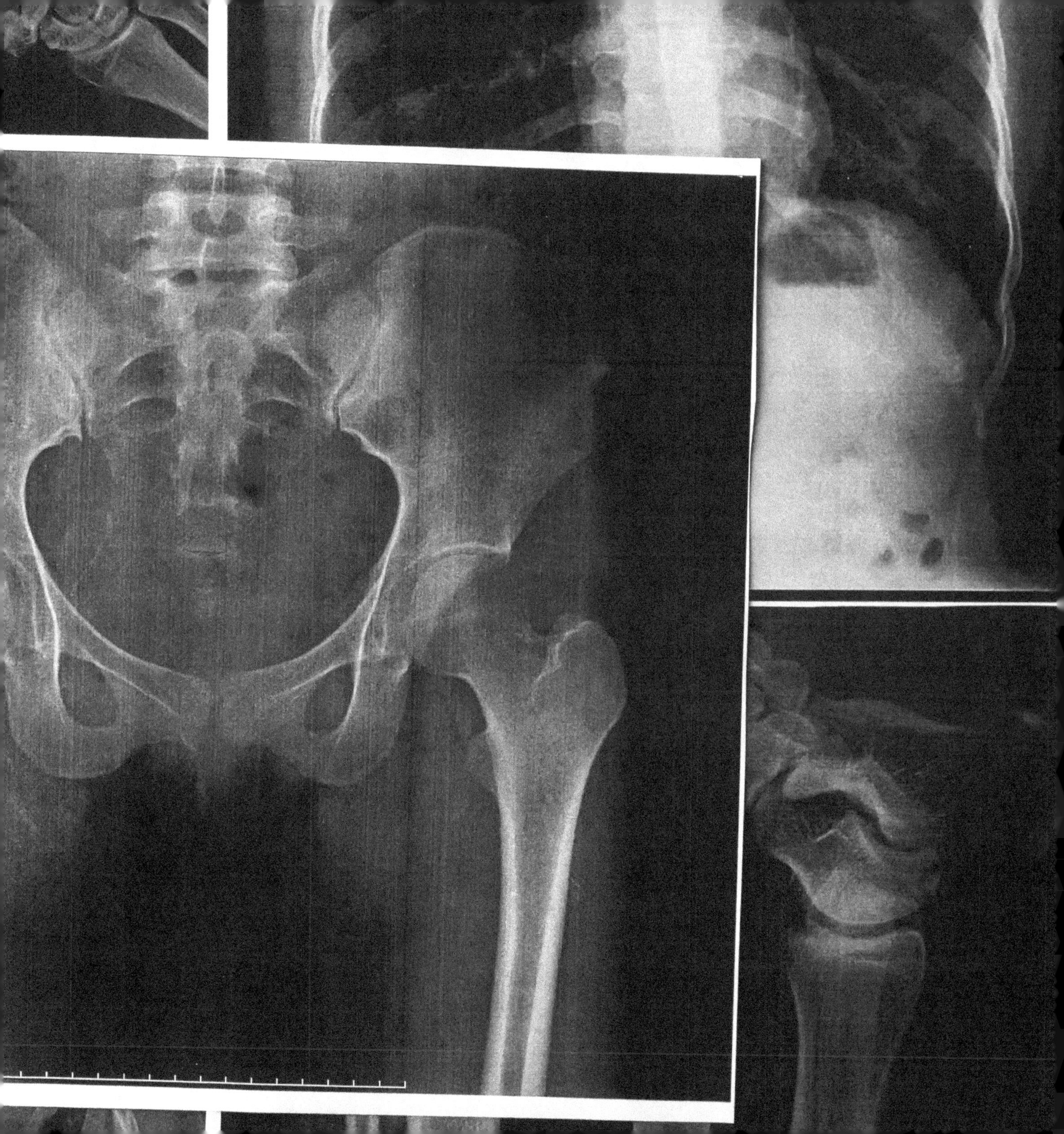

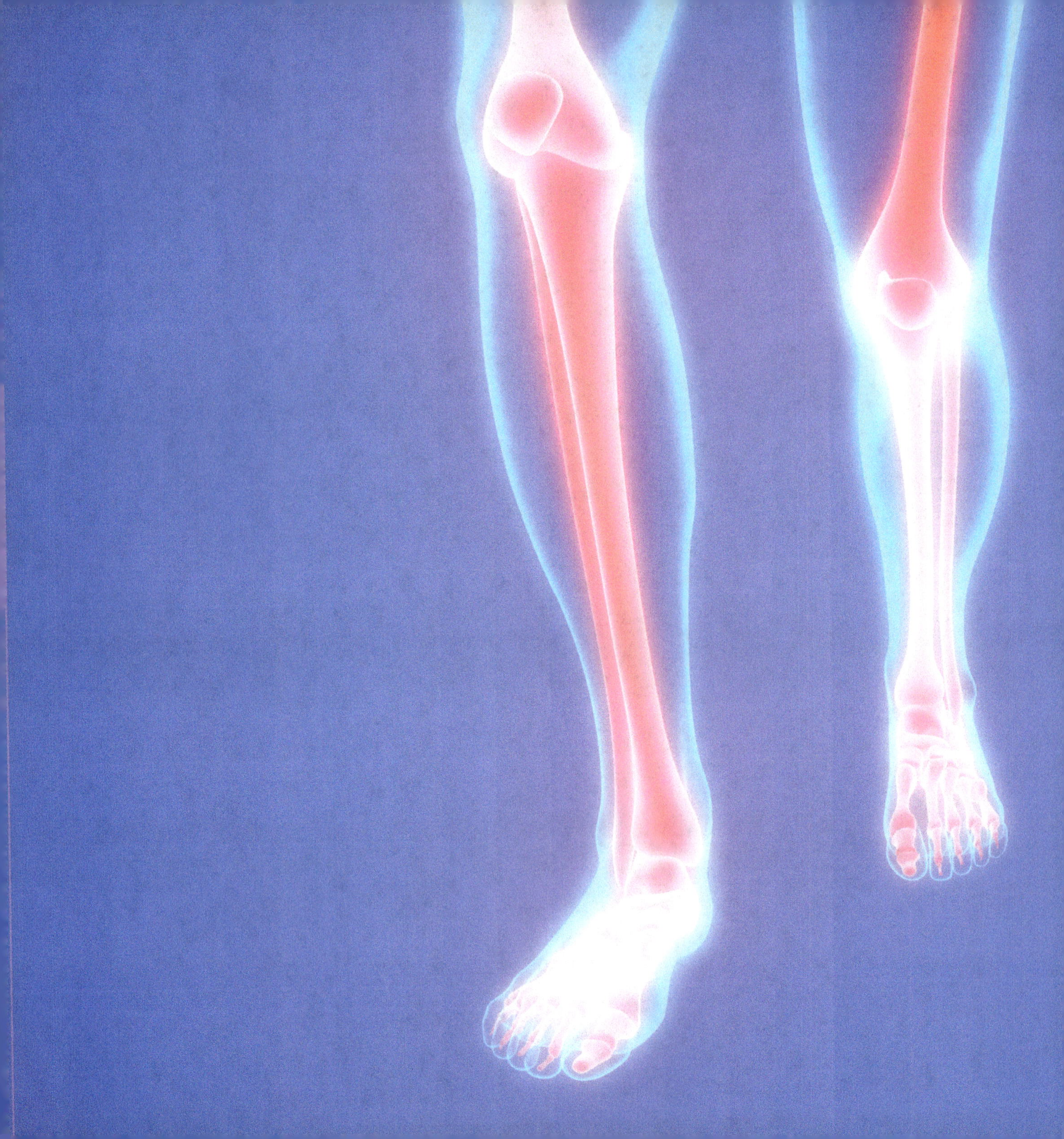

There are two kinds of outer bones in the lower leg between the ankles and the knees. The smaller bone is called the fibula while the larger is known as the tibia. The moveable ball-like front part of the knee is called the patella.

It is essential to keep the bones strong and healthy. Healthy bones continue to help us move around as they provide support for our muscles.

So, eat up and drink different sources of calcium to strengthen your bones!

Visit

www.BabyProfessorBooks.com

to download Free Baby Professor eBooks
and view our catalog of new and exciting
Children's Books